ENHANCING YOUR LEADERSHIP, COMMUNICATION AND PERFORMANCE DNA

DENOLA M BURTON

FOREWORD BY LINDA CLEMONS®
GLOBAL SALES AND NONVERBAL COMMUNICATIONS EXPERT

Denola M. Burton

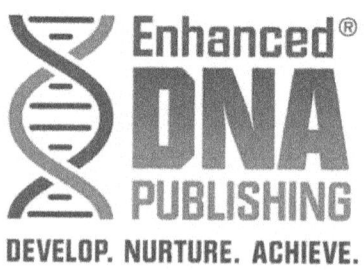

Enhanced DNA Publishing
DenolaBurton@EnhancedDNA1.com
317-537-1438

ENHANCING YOUR LEADERSHIP, COMMUNICATION AND PERFORMANCE DNA
Copyright © 2024 Denola M. Burton

All rights reserved.

No portion of this publication may be reproduced, stored in any electronic system, or transmitted in any form or by any means without the written permission from the author. Brief quotations may be used in literary reviews.

ISBN-13: 979-8-9874187-5-8
Library of Congress Number: 2024921026

DEDICATION

This book is dedicated to all those who have trusted me to DEVELOP and NURTURE their leadership, communication, and performance over the past 30 years as an HR professional and now as an entrepreneur. Your commitment to growth and your journey to ACHIEVE success in both your personal and professional lives have inspired this work.

Denola M. Burton

FOREWORD

By Linda Clemons®
Global Sales and Nonverbal Communications Expert

When it comes to leadership, communication, and body language, I have spent my career transforming clients, helping them generate over two billion dollars in sales. As a body language expert, trained and certified in Analytic Interviewing and Statement Analysis™ - tools used to detect deception - I have had the privilege of coaching some of the top leadership and sales teams around the globe. My work provides me with a unique perspective on how people connect, lead, and ultimately perform at their best. I have always believed that leadership and communication are at the heart of success, and I can confidently say that Denola Burton embodies these principles in ways that are both powerful and transformative.

I first met Denola around 2018 when she was stepping into entrepreneurship. Though new to business ownership, she was not new to her craft. With her deep expertise as an HR professional and a seasoned leader, Denola had already spent years developing leaders, enhancing communication skills, and helping others unlock their true potential. Her authenticity and genuine passion for nurturing others were immediately clear. I knew from our very first encounter that she was not just a consultant or trainer; she was a leader in the truest sense, one who lived her message and delivered measurable, lasting results.

What makes Denola unique is her ability to connect the dots between leadership, communication, and performance in ways that are accessible and actionable. In her book, *Enhancing Your Leadership, Communication, and Performance DNA*, Denola provides a holistic framework designed to elevate your leadership abilities, foster meaningful connections, and enhance your overall performance. This is not a one-size-fits-all approach; rather, it is a tailored guide for personal and professional growth that meets you where you are and helps you evolve.

Denola's framework, which she refers to as "Enhancing Your DNA," is more than just a metaphor. It's a structured, thoughtful process for identifying and nurturing the unique traits that make you a better person, a more effective communicator, and a stronger leader. The DNA she speaks of is your leadership identity - the core of who you are as a leader, how you engage with others, and the lasting impact you leave behind.

In these pages, you'll find practical tools, insightful strategies, and real-world examples that will help you chart a course for your own growth. Whether you are a seasoned leader looking to sharpen your skills or an emerging talent eager to establish your voice, this book offers something invaluable: a roadmap to becoming the best version of yourself. More than that, Denola challenges you to take what you learn and apply it to others, to lift up the people around you as you enhance your own leadership DNA.

As you dive into this book, my hope is that you absorb the lessons and wisdom that Denola has carefully woven throughout. Let this book guide you, not just as a leader or communicator, but as someone committed to growth, impact, and service. Use the tools Denola provides to shape your own path, and in turn, guide others toward their own success. Leadership is not just about reaching your goals; it's about helping others achieve theirs, too. And through this book, you will learn how to do both.

Denola M. Burton

TABLE OF CONTENTS

DEDICATION III
FOREWORD V
INTRODUCTION XI
PART 1: DEVELOP 1
CHAPTER 1: THE FOUNDATION OF PERSONAL AND PROFESSIONAL GROWTH 3
CHAPTER 2: DEVELOPING LEADERSHIP SKILLS 13
CHAPTER 3: DEVELOPING EFFECTIVE COMMUNICATION SKILLS 23
CHAPTER 4: DEVELOPING YOUR EXPERTISE FOR MAXIMUM PERFORMANCE 35
PART 2: NURTURE 43
CHAPTER 5: NURTURING LEADERSHIP GROWTH 45
CHAPTER 6: NURTURING COMMUNICATION SKILLS 51
CHAPTER 7: NURTURING PERFORMANCE – YOURS AND THOSE AROUND YOU 57
PART 3: ACHIEVE 67
CHAPTER 8: ACHIEVING PEAK PERFORMANCE IN LEADERSHIP 69
CHAPTER 9: ACHIEVING EXCELLENCE IN COMMUNICATION 75
CHAPTER 10: ACHIEVING PERFORMANCE EXCELLENCE 77
PART 4: PRACTICAL APPLICATION 83
CHAPTER 11: TAKING ACTION 85
FINAL THOUGHTS 91
ABOUT THE AUTHOR 93

Denola M. Burton

INTRODUCTION

The concept of *Enhancing Your DNA* serves as a framework for personal and professional growth. Just as DNA in the body - deoxyribonucleic acid - is the foundation of who we are biologically, shaping our unique traits and characteristics, our personal and professional DNA is the core of who we are as individuals. DNA carries the instructions for all living things to grow, adapt, and survive, but in the human experience, it is more than just biological; it symbolizes our potential for development and transformation.

At birth, we inherit a set of genetic building blocks that remain unchanged throughout our lives. However, while we cannot alter the fundamental structure of our DNA, we can influence how we develop, nurture, and achieve our goals based on the experiences we have and the knowledge we gain. This is where the concept of *Enhancing Your DNA* comes into play. It's about taking the foundation of who you are and elevating it through continuous learning, intentional nurturing, and relentless pursuit of your objectives.

In the same way that DNA is responsive to environmental factors in the biological sense, our personal and professional DNA is shaped by the experiences we have and how we choose to respond to them. We grow through our challenges, learn from our failures, and find success through our perseverance. Each of these experiences plays a critical role in enhancing who we are.

In this book, you will be guided through the process to **Develop**, **Nurture**, and ultimately **Achieve** your fullest potential in three key areas: Leadership**,** Communication, and Performance. These elements are the lifeblood of both personal and professional success. Whether you are looking to become a more impactful leader, improve your communication with others, or elevate your performance in your career or life, the Enhanced DNA framework will provide the roadmap.

By learning to develop your strengths, nurture the areas that need growth, and achieve your objectives, you will be able to step into your full potential as a leader, communicator, and performer. Enhancing Your DNA means taking control of the elements that you can change and improving upon the ones that are already present.

As you embark on this journey, you'll discover that success is not a destination but a process of continuous growth and refinement. You'll learn to enhance the foundational elements that define you, so you can achieve greatness in both your personal and professional life.

To your growth,
Denola

Enhancing Your Leadership, Communication and Performance DNA

PART 1: DEVELOP

Denola M. Burton

CHAPTER 1: THE FOUNDATION OF PERSONAL AND PROFESSIONAL GROWTH

Personal and professional growth begins with self-awareness and knowing who you are at your core. You need to understand what drives you and how your values shape your decisions. Without this foundation, it is difficult to align your actions with your goals.

The first step to self-awareness to move you toward personal development is to reflect. Reflecting on your values, beliefs and motivations will allow you to gain a deeper understanding of who you are at the core of your being – your DNA.

Assessing Your Values

Values are the guiding principles that shape our thoughts, behaviors, and decisions. They represent the ideals or beliefs that we hold as important or desirable, and they serve as the foundation for how we live our lives, both personally and professionally. Unlike skills or traits, values are deeply ingrained and are often formed through life experiences, upbringing, and culture. They are the compass that directs us in making choices that align with who we are and who we want to become.

Values influence nearly every aspect of our lives. When we are clear about what we value, we can make decisions that are aligned with our core beliefs, leading to a greater sense of fulfillment and purpose. For example, if you value integrity, you will prioritize honesty and transparency in your actions, even when it's difficult. Similarly, if you value growth, you will seek opportunities to learn and improve, both personally and professionally.

Our values also shape the way we interact with others, the type of work we find meaningful, and how we respond to challenges. Values are a key component of self-awareness, because understanding your values helps you stay true to yourself in moments of uncertainty or when faced with difficult decisions.

Self-awareness begins with understanding your core values. There are several ways to discover what values matter most to you:

1. Reflect on Your Experiences: Think about moments when you felt the most fulfilled, proud, or content. What values were being honored in those moments? Similarly, consider times when you felt dissatisfied or conflicted; were any of your values being compromised?

2. Align Your Values with Actions: Once you have identified your core values, examine whether your actions and decisions align with them. Are there areas of your life where you are acting against your values? For example, if you value work-life balance but consistently overwork, it may be time to reassess your approach to your personal and professional life.
3. Seek Feedback from Trusted Sources: Sometimes, those closest to you can offer valuable insights into your values. Ask a trusted friend, mentor, or colleague what they perceive to be your core values based on your behavior and choices. Their perspective may help you uncover values you didn't realize were so central to your life.

Beliefs Shape How We Live Out Our Values

Beliefs are the convictions or ideas we hold to be true about the world, ourselves, and others. These are often formed through our life experiences, upbringing, education, and culture. Beliefs can be conscious (things we actively think about) or subconscious (deep-seated assumptions we might not realize we have).

Our beliefs often determine how we express or prioritize our values. For instance, if someone values achievement, they may believe that "hard work is the only path to success," leading them to focus on diligence and perseverance. On the other hand, if another person values achievement but believes that "success is a balance of work and life," they may pursue success in a more balanced, holistic way.

Though values and beliefs are distinct, they are interwoven. Values influence the kinds of beliefs we adopt, while our beliefs help reinforce or shape our values. Together, they form the core of how we perceive the world and what we prioritize in life.

Reflecting on Values and Beliefs

As part of your personal and professional development journey, take time to reflect on the following:

- What are my core values? Which principles guide my life and decisions?
- What beliefs do I hold about myself and the world? How do they shape my actions?
- Are my values and beliefs aligned? Are there any limiting beliefs that conflict with my values and hold me back?
- How can I live more authentically by aligning my actions with my values and beliefs?

Values and beliefs are essential pillars of self-awareness and personal growth. While values provide the guiding framework for what is important, beliefs give shape to those values, offering the reasoning and context for your actions. Together, they define who you are and help you move forward in your personal and professional journey. By aligning your goals and actions with your values and beliefs, you create a roadmap for authentic, purposeful growth.

Assessing Strengths, Weaknesses, and Growth Areas

To embark on a journey of personal and professional growth, it's essential to assess your strengths, weaknesses, and areas ripe for development. Several effective tools and methods can aid you in this process, each offering unique insights into your capabilities and potential.

Personality or Behavioral Assessments

One of the most insightful ways to understand yourself is through personality or behavior-based assessments. Tools such as the Myers-Briggs Type Indicator (MBTI), CliftonStrengths, and DISC are designed to reveal your personality traits, preferences, and behaviors. These assessments help illuminate why you behave the way you do and how these behaviors influence both your work and personal life. By understanding your personality or behavior-based profile, you can harness your strengths and address any behavioral tendencies that may be limiting your progress.

SWOT Analysis

Another powerful tool is the SWOT (Strengths, Weaknesses, Opportunities, Threats) analysis. While commonly used in business, a personal SWOT analysis can be equally valuable. This method encourages you to identify your internal strengths and weaknesses as well as external opportunities and threats. By examining these aspects, you can uncover blind spots, recognize growth opportunities, and anticipate challenges that may affect your development.

360-Degree Feedback

To gain a comprehensive view of how others perceive you, consider using 360-degree feedback. This approach involves collecting input from colleagues, supervisors, and peers, providing a multi-faceted perspective on your strengths and areas for improvement. Comparing this feedback with your self-assessment can reveal insights into any discrepancies or alignments, offering a clearer understanding of your personal impact and areas for growth.

Adopting a Growth Mindset

Another powerful piece of the puzzle is cultivating a growth mindset. This concept involves the belief that your abilities and intelligence can be developed over time through dedication and effort. Embracing a growth mindset allows you to view challenges as opportunities for learning and encourages perseverance in the face of setbacks. This mindset is fundamental for driving meaningful progress and achieving long-term success.

Goal Setting for Personal and Professional Growth

To achieve any objective, having a structured plan is essential. This ensures that your goals are clear, actionable, and realistic. While the SMART Goals Framework is a widely recommended tool for setting effective objectives, I prefer to enhance it with an additional element, creating what I call SMA<u>A</u>RT Goals. By incorporating this extra "A," you can refine your goal-setting process further. Your goals should be:

1. SPECIFIC: In order for a goal to be effectively met, it must be specific – clearly defined and narrowed down to a point where it is able to be accomplished. To set specific goals, you can answer the following questions:

*Who: Who is involved?
*What: What do I want to accomplish?
*When: Establish a time frame.
*Where: Identify a location.
*Why: Specific reasons, purpose or benefits of accomplishing the goal.

2. MEASURABLE: You must be able to put metrics around your goals – make it quantifiable so that the goal doesn't get lost. I prefer to "chunk" my goals into smaller pieces with shorter timelines and measurements. When you measure your progress, you stay on track, reach your target dates, and experience "intermittent reinforcement" of the ability to reach a goal.

To determine if your goal is measurable, ask questions such as……

- By when?
- How much?
- How many?
- How will I know when it is accomplished?

3. **ATTAINABLE:** It is very important to set goals and measurements that are attainable – able to be achieved. If you set unrealistic goals, you will get discouraged and drop the goal. You can attain most any goal you set when you make a plan and establish a realistic timeframe that allows you to carry out those steps. Goals that may have seemed far away and out of reach eventually move closer and become more attainable, not because your goals shrink, but because you grow and expand to match them.

4. **REALISTIC:** To be realistic, you have to have a sensible and practical idea of what can be achieved or expected. You must be willing and able to get the work done. You must be true to yourself about what you are willing to do to accomplish that goal – you are the only one who can determine how much or how high your goal should be.

5. **TIMELY:** Your goals should be time bound. With no timeframe associated with your goals, you may not have the sense of urgency to complete the goal and you may never complete the goal – it becomes an ongoing project. If you continue to miss the timeframe set,

reevaluate the goal to make sure that you "chunked" it appropriately. Break it down and reset your expectations.

6. Now let's talk about the extra "A" in this acronym. It stands for ACCOUNTABLE: None of the other steps matter if you don't hold yourself accountable! Doing what is required and expected to complete your goals is only important if you recognize the successes and the failures. If your goals are met, celebrate them and if they are not met, call yourself out and regroup! Identify barriers to completing the goal and map out a new plan – chunking the goals, identifying new goals, identifying different metrics or even changing the timeframe if needed.

The SMAART Goals Framework is essential for achieving your objectives because it provides a structured approach to goal-setting that enhances clarity and effectiveness. By incorporating the traditional SMART criteria—Specific, Measurable, Achievable, Relevant, and Time-bound—with an additional "A" for Accountability, the framework ensures that your goals are not only well-defined but also actively tracked and supported. This added focus on accountability helps maintain motivation and commitment, driving consistent progress toward your objectives. The SMAART Framework empowers you to set clear, actionable goals with a practical plan for achieving them, ultimately increasing your chances of success.

Conclusion

The effectiveness of these tools and methods hinges on your willingness to be honest and open with yourself. Approach each process with a readiness to dig deep and accept feedback constructively. Use the insights gained to fuel your growth journey, making informed decisions about where to focus your efforts and how to continue developing your capabilities. As a result, you will be well on your way to personal and professional growth.

CHAPTER 2: DEVELOPING LEADERSHIP SKILLS

Throughout my corporate career in HR, one of my primary roles was to cultivate leadership skills among employees, supervisors, and high-level leaders within the organization. This role involved identifying potential, nurturing growth, and guiding individuals to become effective leaders. As an entrepreneur, I continue to embrace this responsibility, helping others to enhance their leadership capabilities in whatever role they are in.

Effective leadership is not just about holding a position of authority; it's about embodying key traits that inspire, motivate, and drive success. At its core, leadership is fundamentally about influence. True leadership extends beyond mere titles or formal roles within an organization; it revolves around the ability to make a meaningful impact on others. Influence is not determined by hierarchical position or authority; rather, it is measured by the extent to which your actions, words, and behaviors affect the attitudes, behaviors, and decisions of those around you.

Effective leaders harness their influence to inspire, motivate, and guide others toward a shared vision or goal. This impact is shaped by their ability to connect with people on a personal level, build trust, and demonstrate empathy. When a leader influences others positively, they foster a sense of commitment and engagement, encouraging individuals to contribute their best efforts and align with the leader's vision.

Influence is also about leading by example and embodying the values and principles you wish to see in others. It involves actively listening, understanding diverse perspectives, and responding to the needs and concerns of your team. By doing so, you create an environment where people feel valued, respected, and motivated to follow your lead.

Here are five key areas to consider when assessing your level of influence as a leader. Reflect on these questions to evaluate your effectiveness and impact:

1. People of influence add value; both to themselves and to others. How are you adding value in your role? Are you helping others grow while also investing in your personal development?
2. Growing your leadership means growing your influence (and vice versa). How are you actively increasing your level of influence? What steps are you taking every day to grow and stretch beyond your current capabilities?

3. As a leader, you attract 'who you are' not 'who you want'. Consider the characteristics of the people you want to lead or influence. To attract those individuals, you must embody the qualities they admire. Are you demonstrating the characteristics of the people you want to attract?
4. Your influence is most impactful when people need it most. Great leaders have a sense for teachable moments and breakthroughs. They recognize when change is possible and necessary, then take action. Are you honing your ability to recognize opportunities for meaningful influence and leadership?
5. Clarify your motives for wanting to lead. Leadership is built on trust and respect. If your motives are genuine, your leadership will naturally be more effective. Have you earned the trust of those you lead? Are your intentions sincere?

Everyone influences someone, but the true question is whether your influence is positive. Reflect on the questions above to gauge your influence and determine if you're an effective leader. When you inspire and positively impact others, you're not just a leader. You're an effective one!

In essence, leadership is not solely about directing or commanding; it is about inspiring and guiding others through your impact. The ability to influence effectively requires a deep understanding of human behavior, strong interpersonal skills, and a genuine commitment to the growth and success of those you lead. Through this positive influence, leaders can drive change, achieve collective goals, and build a legacy of meaningful impact.

Did you know?

- While 83% of employers agree that it's crucial to develop leaders at all levels, only 5% of businesses actually provide integrated leadership development. (Business Insider)
- Only 14% of CEOs have the leadership talent they need to grow their businesses. (Builtin)
- 38% of new leaders fail within the first 18 months. (HBR)
- Organizations that focus on leadership development outperform those that don't by up to 18% in revenue growth. (Gartner)
- Poor leadership is the number one reason why employees quit their jobs, with 50% of employees leaving because of their managers. (Gallup)

Leadership development is widely recognized as essential for organizational success, yet many businesses fail to invest in it effectively. This lack of focus leads to a significant gap in leadership talent, with new leaders struggling to succeed and many employees citing poor leadership as the main reason for leaving their jobs. However, organizations that prioritize leadership development not only improve their internal leadership capabilities but also experience enhanced business growth and employee retention. The message is clear:

developing strong leaders is crucial for long-term success and employee satisfaction.

Now let's explore the essential leadership traits that contribute to successful leadership. By understanding and developing these traits, you can strengthen your leadership skills and positively impact your organization, your team and yourself.

Vision

Leaders must be visionary thinkers. The ability to see the big picture and envision a compelling future for the team or organization is critical. Visionary leaders inspire others with their forward-thinking ideas and planning. In order to create a vision that inspires others to follow, the leader must identify a purpose that is impactful and bigger than any one person.

Strategy

Just like visionaries, leaders must also be strategic thinkers. They must have the ability to analyze complex situations, anticipate future trends and develop long-term plans. Strategic leaders also align their actions with the overall goals and objectives of the organization.

Integrity

Effective leaders operate with integrity, adhering to strong moral and ethical principles. Leaders with integrity build trust, foster respect and establish integrity with their teams by being honest, transparent, consistent and authentic.

Emotional Intelligence

Leaders must understand and manage their own emotions as well as recognizing and influencing the emotions of others. Effective leaders lead by example and demonstrate empathy, self-management and social skills.

Communication

Leaders must have the ability to clearly articulate ideas and engage in meaningful dialogue as well as having the skill to demonstrate active listening skills. Effective communication helps in conveying expectations, providing feedback and fostering collaboration.

In today's competitive professional landscape, possessing strong leadership skills is crucial for success. Cultivating these skills enables leaders to inspire and guide their teams effectively, fostering an environment that promotes productivity, collaboration, and personal growth. By developing and refining these capabilities, leaders not only drive their teams toward achieving organizational goals but also contribute to long-term success. Investing in your leadership development unlocks your full potential, empowering you to make a significant impact and excel both personally and professionally.

Developing Critical Thinking and Problem-Solving Skills

While developing your area of expertise is essential, it's equally important to cultivate complementary skills like critical thinking and problem-solving. These foundational skills are indispensable across all levels of leadership, communication, and performance. Mastering them can significantly enhance your ability to lead effectively, communicate clearly, and solve complex challenges in a fast-paced and evolving workplace.

The Importance of Critical Thinking

Critical thinking is the ability to analyze and evaluate information to make reasoned judgements. You need to have the ability to critically assess situations and make informed decisions which will have a direct impact on both team and organizational outcomes. Developing critical thinking ensures that you can navigate complex issues, challenge assumptions and eventually make strategic decisions.

Action Step: Practice critical thinking by questioning your own assumptions. When faced with a decision, ask yourself, "What is another way to approach this problem?" The more you practice this, the more you will be effective with your critical thinking skills.

Enhancing Your Problem-Solving Abilities

Problem-solving aligns with critical thinking but involves taking a more active approach to addressing specific challenges. You may be faced with unpredictable obstacles and being a proficient problem-solver means you can think quickly and creatively to find solutions that benefit those you are working with.

It is important to not just treat the symptoms of a problem, it is important to identify the root cause of the problem. This ensures that the solutions you identify are sustainable and you are identifying underlying issues. As you identify those root causes, it is important to generate innovative solutions. Rather than defaulting to conventional methods, a good problem-solver uses critical thinking to give a competitive edge. And as you identify solutions, you must adapt to changing conditions because the best solutions may not always be immediately obvious which means you need to be flexible and prepared when new information arises.

Action Step: Take time to gather relevant data and consult others before jumping to conclusions. Consider a range of solutions, evaluate their potential impacts and then test your hypothesis prior to implementing.

Building these skills at Every Level

Whether you're an emerging leader or an experienced executive, critical thinking and problem-solving are skills that can be continuously refined and applied at all levels of leadership, communication, and performance.

- At the individual level: These skills will help you better manage your own tasks and responsibilities. When faced with challenges, you'll be able to think more independently and take initiative in solving problems without relying on external direction.

- At the team level: As a leader, critical thinking helps you assess team dynamics, understand different personalities, and solve interpersonal conflicts. Problem-solving allows you to coach your team through challenges and empower them to find solutions, fostering a collaborative culture.

- At the organizational level: At higher levels of leadership, these skills are crucial for strategic planning, navigating complex projects, and driving organizational change. As a leader, you'll be tasked with identifying systemic issues and designing large-scale solutions that impact the entire company.

Conclusion

- In Leadership: Leaders with strong critical thinking skills inspire trust and confidence in their teams. When you thoughtfully assess situations and present well-reasoned solutions, your team will see you as a reliable decision-maker.

- In Communication: Critical thinking enhances your ability to articulate your ideas clearly and persuasively. Problem-solving allows you to frame challenges in ways that encourage constructive dialogue rather than creating tension.

- In Performance: Critical thinking enables you to continuously assess your own performance, identify areas for improvement, and develop solutions to enhance productivity and effectiveness.

Denola M. Burton

CHAPTER 3: DEVELOPING EFFECTIVE COMMUNICATION SKILLS

Mastering effective communication skills is crucial for unlocking opportunities and building connections. Over the years, I have learned that conveying my thoughts, feelings and ideas concisely and with impact have impacted my ability to unlock doors, build connections and shape my personal and professional life. In this chapter we will focus on the main types of communication: verbal communication, non-verbal communication, written communication and visual communication. However, communication is not complete if we don't include active listening, digital communication and the impact on interpersonal communication.

Verbal Communication

In its simplest form, verbal communication is oral communication – what we speak aloud. Oral communication cannot be effective unless it is between two or more people. Verbal communication is the foundation for effective communication and is essential in everyday life, playing a crucial role in fostering collaboration and cultivating relationships and it is important that verbal communication goes both ways in order for it to be effective. You and the person receiving the message must understand each other for this communication to be effective.

Verbal communication skills range from the obvious (being able to speak clearly, or listening, for example), to the more subtle (such as reflecting and clarifying) and is ideal for face-to-face interactions, team meetings, brainstorming sessions, and situations that require immediate feedback and emotional connection.

Non-verbal Communication

Nonverbal communication is the transmission of messages or signals through a nonverbal platform such as eye contact, body language, touch, voice, physical appearance, and/or use of objects. Non-verbal communication encompasses aspects of communication other than spoken or written words. It includes elements such as tone, pitch, and body movements which significantly influence how messages are perceived.

Here are some types of nonverbal communication and the effects they can have on the success of your communication:
- Facial expressions: Your facial expression can communicate a message that can align or contradict with the words you are saying. Facial expressions; happy, sad, angry; help you convey your message but

it is important to be aware of your facial expression when you talk and particularly when you listen, which is when it is easy to forget to control your expressions. This is most important when you hear (or are sharing) a message that you don't necessarily agree with.

- Gestures: When you speak, a gesture can make your message stronger. Pointing out something you want your listener to look at more closely is an example of nonverbal communication that makes your message understood. Motioning warmly toward a coworker who deserves special recognition, making a fist to show frustration or anger, such gestures help further engage your audience or help them receive the appropriate message when you speak.

- Proximity: How close you are to your audience when you speak sends another nonverbal message. If your size is imposing and you leave a very small distance between you and your listener, it is likely your nonverbal communication could be viewed as intimidating or threatening. On the other hand, giving someone too much space is an awkward nonverbal communication that might confuse your listener and make them question your motive.

- Touch: Shaking a hand or putting your hand on a shoulder are examples of nonverbal cues that can affect the success or impact of your message. Touch communicates affection, but it also communicates power. You may have formed an impression about someone who shook your hand with a weak handshake versus a firm one, even if the words they said may have sounded confident.

- Eye contact: Making and maintaining eye contact with a person or an audience when you're verbally communicating or listening communicates to the other party that you are interested and engaged in the conversation. Good eye contact often conveys the trait of honesty to the other party.

- Appearance: Your clothing, hair, and overall appearance are also a part of nonverbal communication. The quality, condition or appropriateness of your clothing can be potential cues that speak nonverbally about you as a person or communicator. Whether rightly or wrongly, these are things that people may subconsciously think as we interact with them.

I recently recalled a scenario on social media where a young lady went to an interview in a "shorts set". The shorts set appeared to be very neat and clean, however, the interviewer asked her to reconsider her attire and allowed her to return home to change clothes. The young lady, in her description in her post, stressed that since she was neat, the interviewer should not have had any issue with her attire. Many people commented on her post that there were certain standards for interviewing and unless she was aware that the place she was interviewing embraced that attire, she should have been dressed more "professionally". What do you think?

Nonverbal communication reveals a lot about you and how you relate to other people. It pays to be aware of the elements of your nonverbal communication so you can maximize the impact of your message. Remember that nonverbal communication is essential when conveying emotions, emphasizing points, and influencing how your message is received. It is particularly crucial in negotiations, presentations, and public speaking.

Written Communication

Written communication is any written message that two or more people exchange. Written communication is typically more formal but can be less efficient than oral communication. Written communication is a structured and permanent form of communication, often used in formal and professional settings. It is the most common form of business communication and has become increasingly important throughout the information age we live in. Written communications can take place traditionally on paper or more modern methods such as on an electronic device, such as by email or electronic memo.

For effective written communication, I always follow the 5 C's of communication: clear, cohesive, complete, concise, and concrete.

- Be **Clear** about your message. All written communications should be clear, direct, straightforward, and understandable. Confusion will be prevented amongst readers if the message makes sense.

- Be **Cohesive** by staying on-topic. Written communications should be kept short to avoid repetition and avoid leaving out necessary information. Conciseness assists in making a message more clear.

- **Complete** your idea with supporting content. All necessary information should be included in the written communication

- Be **Concise** by eliminating unnecessary words. Written communications should be kept short to avoid repetition and avoid leaving out necessary information. Conciseness assists in making a message more clear.

- Be **Concrete** by using precise words. All facts and dates should be accurate, and all spelling and grammar should also be correct. Precision builds a professional tone and confirms effective research has been done.

The 5 C's will help improve the effectiveness of your written communication. Of course, these principles also apply to verbal communication, where things like body language and eye contact can sometimes muddle a message.

Visual Communication

Visual communication relies on images, symbols, and graphics to convey messages. It is a powerful tool in sales, marketing, design, and data representation. Visual communication is very effective in presentations, sales pitches, data analysis, and any other situations where information needs to be conveyed rapidly and memorably.

Communication is a skill that can be gently nurtured and enhanced by exploring the different ways we express ourselves. Whether through spoken words, the nuances of body language, the clarity of writing, or the power of visual elements, becoming comfortable with these various forms of communication can help you connect more meaningfully, influence others positively, and succeed in your personal and professional life.

Here are some tips for improving your communication skills whether verbal, non-verbal, written or visual.

> 1. Consider your message: Decide what you want to convey during your next conversation, written communication or presentation. This might involve brainstorming or outlining a list of key points you'd like to make. By reviewing the information you want to share, you can be sure your follow the 5 C's.

2. Recognize your audience: Keep your intended audience in mind when communicating and consider their perspective. Your intended audience will dictate the tone of the communication as well as the mannerisms and other aspects of verbal communication you can use to enhance your communication. For example, it may be appropriate to use a warm and familiar tone with a friend, family member or even a coworker, but a new client or an executive may expect a more formal presentation of your thoughts and ideas.

3. Be mindful of your nonverbal communication: When you are communicating through spoken word, you should always pay attention to any nonverbal cues you might be portraying. This includes actions like eye contact, posture, laughing, coughing, yawning and facial expressions. Being aware of your nonverbal communication ensures that the message you convey through your actions or body language matches the message you convey through your words.

4. Speak clearly: Think about how you want to speak before you begin. Regulate your breathing so that it remains steady while you talk and consider how quickly or slowly you need to talk. Speaking clearly can improve how well others understand you and ensure that the words you say come through and remain with your audience. One of the most important aspects of speaking clearly is adapting to your audience, the setting

and the message so that your tone matches the information you want to share.

5. Choose your written words carefully: Just as you would speak clearly, you would also write with clear intent. Using an outline, for example, will help you stay focused on your topic. But you will also want to choose words and phrases that are appropriate for your intended audience. In addition, you'll want to make sure that your written communication is not too long or filled with unnecessary detail.

6. Practice active listening: Know when to stop speaking when you are "the sender" and prepare to listen as you become "the receiver" when the other party is speaking. Active listening will ensure that the sender and receiver are equally exchanging messages and feedback.

7. Think before you hit 'reply': This might be considered the written equivalent of active listening, but it's important to think before you reply in writing, especially if the topic is something that is causing confusion or debate.

Active Listening

Active listening is a deliberate and conscious effort to truly hear and understand the speaker's message whether the communication is verbal or non-verbal. By actively listening, you gain a better understanding of the message, build or maintain trust with those you are communicating with and can reduce misunderstandings in personal and professional relationships.

To actively listen, you need to provide your full attention to the speaker, giving them your full attention. This is best done by avoiding distractions and showing the speaker that you are listening through verbal acknowledgements and even non-verbal cues (body language).

The benefit of active listening is enhancing the relationships of those you are communicating with. By demonstrating that you are truly interested in what the speaker is communicating, you are promoting deeper and more meaningful communications with others. It also helps in addressing and resolving conflicts by gaining understanding of all perspectives. Active listening also facilitates better teamwork and cooperation by ensuring all voices are heard and valued.

Conclusion

This chapter delved into the four primary modes of communication: verbal, non-verbal, written, and visual, each playing a vital role in how we connect and convey messages. It also focused on the fact that communication is more that talking or writing, you also must be an active listener to effectively communicate. Using these various forms of communication gives you a complete toolkit for sharing ideas, building relationships, and succeeding in different areas of life. Mastering each type allows you to engage in more effective and impactful interactions.

Denola M. Burton

CHAPTER 4: DEVELOPING YOUR EXPERTISE FOR MAXIMUM PERFORMANCE

The most effective way to develop your expertise for maximum performance is to continually build your knowledge and skills in a focused area. Expertise doesn't happen overnight; it requires intentional learning, practice and the discipline to deep dive into a specific area. You need to continually establish yourself as an expert by actively seeking opportunities to expand your understanding by immersing yourself in your chosen field. Expertise is not just about what you know, it's about applying that knowledge in meaningful ways that drive better performance, fosters innovation and distinguishes you as a leader in your specific space.

Identifying your Area of Expertise

Developing your area of expertise starts with narrowing your focus to a specific topic or area. This will help cultivate depth and credibility in a subject matter. If you do not already have an established area of expertise, reflect on the following:

- What topics energize you? What are you passionate about? What subjects intrigue you? Which areas do you naturally gravitate to in your professional and personal life?

- Think about past projects or activities where you felt most engaged or fulfilled. Reflect on these projects or activities to determine if you have the knowledge or skills to develop the topic as your expertise.

- Where do you see gaps in the marketplace, industry or field that align with your passions? What problems are you uniquely positioned to solve?

Action Step: Write down three areas of interest or passion that you are excited to explore further.

Building Knowledge and Skills

Once you identify the area of expertise that you want to develop, then you need to determine whether you need to obtain additional education or knowledge in that area or whether you need to obtain certain certifications to be identified as an expert in that field.

- Reflect on what you already know and identify any key insights, skills or knowledge that make you stand out in this area.

- How have you applied this knowledge in real-world situations? Think about specific projects, initiatives or problems you have previously solved using this expertise.

- You can also consider the feedback that you have received from others about your strengths and contributions in this area. Peer recognition can help identify where you have already established expertise.

Action Step: List three to five achievements or experiences that showcase your existing expertise and how it has impacted others.

Own Your Expertise

- Once you have established a foundation in your area of expertise, it is time to position yourself as a thought leader. Share your knowledge through writing, speaking engagements, workshops, or online platforms.
- Build a personal brand that communicates your expertise clearly and effectively. What value can you provide to others through your knowledge?
- Be confident in promoting your skills and sharing your insights, and don't hesitate to seek opportunities where you can demonstrate your knowledge.

Action step: Develop a strategy for sharing your expertise with a broader audience through content creation, networking or even public speaking.

Conclusion

I remember a pivotal moment in my corporate career as a scientist when I was asked to take on a short-term assignment in Human Resources (HR). At the time, I knew little about HR, but I was eager to learn since the goal was to bring those HR skills back into my business area. What surprised me, however, was how much I fell in love with the field. HR was more than just a temporary assignment; it became a passion, and I knew that if I wanted to thrive in this new area, I had to establish myself as a credible HR professional.

What excited me most about HR was the opportunity to develop and nurture others, helping them grow and succeed in their roles. This motivation drove me to build expertise in the field. I began by researching the tools available that could help me grow my knowledge and use that knowledge to make an impact in the business I supported. I knew that to be seen as an expert, I needed more than enthusiasm but also credibility.

So, I became a student of the field. I joined the Society for Human Resource Management (SHRM), the world's largest HR association, which equips professionals with knowledge, resources, and support to create better workplaces. I immersed myself in the local IndySHRM community and attended their conferences, including the national SHRM annual conferences. These experiences deepened my understanding of HR trends and best practices, and I dedicated myself to mastering this new area of focus.

To solidify my expertise, I pursued and successfully obtained the SHRM-PHR (Professional in Human Resources) certification, a credential offered by the Human Resources Certification Institute (HRCI). This was a major milestone in building my credibility as an HR professional, but I knew I wanted to specialize further.

I sought a role in Employee Relations within my company—a position that allowed me to focus on improving communication between management and employees while effectively resolving workplace conflicts. This role was crucial in fostering a positive organizational culture, and it aligned perfectly with my passion for supporting individuals and teams.

For over two decades, my focus remained on creating positive, lasting impacts in both individuals and organizations. In 2012, I was honored to receive the "HR Impact" award, voted on by HR leadership and peers, a recognition that underscored the contributions I made in the organization and in the field.

Measuring and Reflecting on Your Progress

Once you've developed your expertise, measuring and reflecting on your progress is critical to ensuring continued growth and effectiveness. Here are some key steps to help you assess where you stand and plan your next steps:

Set Clear and Measurable Goals

The first step in measuring progress is to set specific, measurable, achievable, actionable, relevant, and time-bound (SMAART) goals for yourself (discussed in Chapter 1). These goals should align with your area of expertise and represent key milestones that you want to achieve. Whether it's mastering a new tool, completing a certification, or improving performance in a specific role, clear goals give you a benchmark to measure your growth.

Action Step: Break your long-term goals into smaller, actionable tasks and check your progress against these milestones regularly. Review whether you're meeting deadlines and achieving the desired outcomes.

Engage in Self-Reflection

Self-reflection is a critical aspect of assessing your expertise. Take time to look back on your journey, evaluate how far you've come, and think about what you've learned. Consider not only your accomplishments but also the challenges you've faced and how you've overcome them.

Action Step: At regular intervals (monthly or quarterly), set aside time to reflect on your achievements and setbacks. Ask yourself questions like: "What have I learned over the past few months?" and "How have I grown in my expertise?" Journaling can be a useful tool to document your reflections.

Seek Regular Feedback from Others

One of the most effective ways to gauge your progress is through feedback. Constructive feedback can provide you with an external perspective on how well you are applying your expertise. It also helps you identify blind spots and areas of improvement.

Action Step: Schedule regular feedback sessions with trusted colleagues, mentors or other experts in your field. Ask open-ended question to receive both positive and constructive feedback. Remember, "Feedback is a Gift" and you should always accept feedback even if you don't agree with it. You can always reflect to determine if the feedback is relevant and needs action.

Maintaining Expertise and Staying Relevant

True expertise is often measured by the value and impact you bring to others. Whether you're improving team performance, developing innovative solutions, or driving business results, your ability to contribute meaningfully to others and the organization is a key indicator of your progress.

Expertise is not static. To remain an expert, you need to keep up with industry trends, new developments, and emerging technologies or methodologies. Staying current ensures that your knowledge is always relevant and that you can continue to provide value in a rapidly changing environment.

Action Step: Evaluate the outcomes of your work. Are you influencing others positively? Are you helping to solve key challenges in your organization or field? Regularly measure the tangible results of your expertise and adjust your approach based on what drives the most value.

Action Step: Subscribe to industry newsletters, attend conferences, or enroll in ongoing training or certifications.

Celebrate Your Successes

Regularly evaluate how current your knowledge is and look for ways to keep your skills up-to-date.

Recognizing your achievements along the way is critical for maintaining motivation and momentum. Celebrate key milestones, no matter how small, and reward yourself for the progress you've made. Acknowledging your wins helps solidify your growth and reminds you of your hard-earned progress.

Action Step: When you reach a significant goal or achieve a new level of expertise, take time to celebrate. Whether it's a personal reward or recognition from your peers, acknowledging your success is essential to staying engaged and motivated. Don't forget to include others who have been critical to that milestone in your celebration. This could include mentors, coaches and even accountability partners.

By consistently measuring and reflecting on your progress using these steps, you ensure that you stay on track with your personal and professional development, maintain your expertise, and continue to grow over time.

PART 2: NURTURE

Denola M. Burton

CHAPTER 5: NURTURING LEADERSHIP GROWTH

As a leader, continuous learning and development are essential components of your growth and the growth of others around you. When you actively seek opportunities for growth, you broaden your knowledge and you not only strengthen your leadership capabilities, you position yourself as a role model for others. This is the foundation of nurturing where you develop your own potential while simultaneously invest in the growth of others. When you mentor, coach and nurture others, you create a ripple effect that transforms others into empowered and effective leaders.

Nurturing others is more about developing skills, it is about fostering an environment of trust, respect and encouragement where others can thrive. This is the concept of leading by example and demonstrating a commitment to both self-improvement and improvement of others around you. Ultimately, this reciprocal nature of learning creates a cycle of learning and growth that ensures that leadership is not confined to a single individual but as a result strengthens the entire organization.

Becoming a Nurturing Leader

You may have heard many times that employees are a company's most valuable asset. When leaders nurture employees, it can lead to increased job satisfaction, better engagement, and ultimately, higher levels of productivity. Nurturing leaders understand the importance of nurturing employees and how nurturing others can enhance the culture of support and growth.

Here are five things that nurturing leaders do well:

- Nurturing leaders provide clear expectations and help set realistic goals and objectives. Performance standards and expectations are well-defined. When employees understand expectations and performance metrics, they are more likely to feel motivated and engaged in their work.

- Nurturing leaders recognize and reward performance. Listening to employees regarding the type of recognition they prefer is very important. Not all recognition involves money. Sometimes something as simple as expressing gratitude for a job well-done or extra effort can make the difference between a supervisor and a nurturing leader.

- Nurturing leaders offer and provide opportunities for growth and development. This can include training, but many times involved mentoring and coaching. When employees are given the opportunity to learn and develop skills, they are more likely to feel valued with the organization.

- Nurturing leaders create a positive work environment. They create a culture of respect, trust, collaboration and are more likely to attract and retain talented employees. A positive work environment can lead to higher levels of job satisfaction, increased productivity and ultimately reduce turnover.

- Nurturing leaders lead by example. Leading by example models the behavior you want to see in your employees, those you mentors and those around you. When you lead by example, you demonstrate excellence and others will want to emulate that excellence.

Mentoring and Coaching to Enhance Leadership Skills

Mentoring and coaching others helps leaders sharpen their own leadership skills. To effectively mentor or coach, leaders must practice active listening, empathy, communication – all skills which are critical for leadership success. If this occurs, leaders will grow alongside their mentees or coaches as they reflect and share their own experiences. I can recall several relationships where I served as the mentor and yet, I feel like I gained as much value from the relationship as the person I was mentoring and as a result, added to my own personal growth.

Mentoring and coaching helps build deeper relationships

between leaders and those they lead. By investing time and energy into someone's development, leaders demonstrate a genuine interest in their growth. This strengthens trust, respect and loyalty which enhances employee engagement, job satisfaction and less turnover. When leaders actively mentor and coach, they ultimately foster a culture of continuous learning and development. Employees see that growth is valued and supported allowing them to seek out learning opportunities, take on new challenges and pursue personal and professional development. As a result, leaders build deeper relationships building a dynamic and forward-thinking organization.

Encouraging a Leadership Mindset

What is a "leadership mindset"? A leadership mindset is one where leaders have certain attitudes, beliefs and expectations that create the foundation of who you are and how you lead and interact with others. A leadership mindset affects everything that you do – it governs your opinions, decisions, actions and it impact everyone around you. It impacts the relationships that you have, how you achieve your goals and how you operate daily.

The key components of having a leadership mindset include clarity in who you are as a leader and where you want to go. You begin to operate with self-confidence where you become more decisive and have a "can-do" attitude - especially when faced with obstacles. When you have a leadership mindset, you develop and demonstrate excellent communication skills - not just communicating, but also connecting with others. You listen to understand and not just to respond which allows you to take your communication to the next level. And, you begin to identify, manage and demonstrate a high level of emotional intelligence. The more you strengthen your leadership attitude, the easier it will be for you to understand, manage and control your emotions.

Denola M. Burton

CHAPTER 6: NURTURING COMMUNICATION SKILLS

In Chapter 3 we discussed the keys to mastering communication skills. In this chapter, we will expand on communication skills and discuss how you can nurture the current skills you have to enhance your ability to not just communicate but connect to have effective relationships in your personal as well as your professional life.

Building Rapport and Trust

Building rapport and trust is essential for effective communication and cultivating strong relationships. When interacting with others, it's important to show genuine interest in both the person and what they're expressing. Engaging fully in the conversation, free from distractions, signals that you value the exchange. One common distraction is formulating your response while the other person is still talking. This habit can prevent you from fully absorbing what's being said. Instead, focus entirely on the speaker, allowing yourself to be present and attentive.

By giving your full attention and limiting distractions, you demonstrate a commitment to the conversation and engage in active listening. Once the speaker has finished, you can acknowledge their message before crafting your response. Using both verbal and nonverbal cues like nodding, paraphrasing, or affirming statements reinforces that you've heard and understood them. Even if you don't necessarily agree with their point of view, you can still validate their feelings and perspective.

When you establish yourself as an active listener and create space for others to share their thoughts, you foster a deeper connection. This not only builds rapport but also lays the foundation for trust and mutual respect, ensuring that future interactions are constructive and open.

Persuasion and Influence

The art of persuasive communication is a critical aspect of leadership, whether you hold a formal leadership role. Many professionals find themselves in positions where they need to influence others without directly leading a team. While expertise and knowledge play a significant role in establishing credibility, the true power of influence comes from the ability to communicate effectively and authentically—without resorting to manipulation.

Persuasion is about guiding others toward decisions and actions through trust, clarity, and mutual respect. It involves understanding the needs, motivations, and concerns of your audience, allowing you to tailor your message in a way that resonates with them. This requires emotional intelligence, as well as an ability to listen actively and empathize with differing perspectives. By framing your message in terms of shared goals and aligning with the values of those you seek to influence, you foster collaboration rather than coercion.

Successful persuasion is also built on consistency and integrity. People are more likely to be influenced when they trust that your actions align with your words. The goal of true influence is not just to achieve short-term outcomes but to create lasting, positive relationships where mutual benefit is prioritized. Ultimately, effective persuasion empowers others to make informed choices and feel ownership over the direction they take, enhancing both individual and collective success.

Cross-Cultural Communication

Cross-Cultural communication is essential in leadership, especially in today's diverse and globalized work environments. It is important to first of all understand cultural differences, educating yourself about different cultural norms, values and communication styles. Many of us tend to judge others through the lens of our own background, experiences and culture. It is important to keep an open mind and attempt to understand different cultures.

For example, if you are a leader who will be interviewing candidates for a vacant position, these are some of the things you may need to consider:

- Be aware of your own culture, behaviors and biases.

- Recognize cultural nuances since what works in one culture may not work in another.

- Plan to tweak or adjust your tactics, demeanor, approach, tone, language, body language, etc. once you realize that a culture may be different from yours.

- Ensure that the person being interviewed is comfortable, asking questions to determine if there is anything that needs to be adjusted.

These interviewing strategies can be used for any communication scenario or situation when you realize that you are communicating with someone from a different or unfamiliar culture from yours.

Adaptability in Communication

Just as it is important to be aware of cultural differences, leaders must have the ability to adapt their communication style to suit different platforms, contexts, and situations. Mastering adaptability in communication is crucial for overcoming the fear of the unknown. When done effectively, it allows leaders to remain engaged, motivated, and open to change, rather than feeling discouraged or resistant. Strong leaders are willing to adjust their communication approach based on audience feedback, the specific context, and the expectations of the situation. Tailoring communication is essential to achieving desired outcomes.

A clear example of the necessity for adaptable

communication arose during the 2020 pandemic. The global shift forced everyone from students to employees to rethink how we interacted. As quarantine measures took effect, work-from-home became the norm for non-essential workers, and e-learning became standard for students. Training sessions, meetings, and workshops moved online, making tools like Zoom a household name. We had to embrace new technologies rapidly to maintain connection and communication. In many ways, those communication methods have persisted in our post-pandemic world, demonstrating the power and necessity of adaptability in communication.

Conclusion

This chapter highlights the importance of nurturing communication skills for effective leadership, emphasizing building rapport and trust by actively listening and showing genuine interest, which fosters stronger relationships. The ability to persuade and influence others without manipulation is crucial for guiding teams toward shared goals. Leaders must also be aware of cultural differences and adapt their communication styles to avoid misunderstandings and promote inclusivity. Finally, adaptability in communication is key, as leaders must adjust their approach based on audience, feedback, and context to successfully navigate challenges and achieve desired outcomes.

Denola M. Burton

CHAPTER 7: NURTURING PERFORMANCE – YOURS AND THOSE AROUND YOU

Performance is not just about achieving short-term wins or meeting daily goals; it's about cultivating habits and strategies that lead to sustained success over time. Whether you're a leader, a professional striving to grow, or an individual looking to improve, nurturing performance requires a deliberate and structured approach. This chapter will explore the essential components of fostering performance, from organizing your work environment to developing intentional growth strategies. We will also dive into the importance of receiving and giving constructive feedback, learning from top performers in your field, and leveraging the power of mentoring and coaching. By incorporating these elements into your daily practice, you can enhance your productivity, drive success, and ensure continuous improvement. Let's begin by understanding how each of these practices can help you nurture your performance for long-term success.

Utilize Organization Processes

Staying organized is key to staying on top of your work

activities, and utilizing effective organizational tools can help streamline tasks and boost productivity. This begins with setting aside intentional time to organize both your physical and digital workspaces. Your physical desk, inbox, file storage systems, and task management systems are all vital areas that need to be structured for efficiency.

Action Step: Start by decluttering your physical desk to create a workspace that minimizes distractions. Organize important documents and tools in easily accessible locations, ensuring everything has its place.

Action Step: Turn to your virtual environment and organize your inbox, folders, and file storage which will help reduce time wasted searching for emails or documents. Establish clear file-naming conventions and folder structures that you and your team can follow consistently.

Task management systems are invaluable for staying on top of deadlines and responsibilities. Whether you use digital tools such as project management apps, calendars, or traditional to-do lists, having a clear method of tracking your tasks will allow you to prioritize and delegate work more effectively.

Being organized requires both time and persistence, but the return on investment is significant. By committing to organizing and maintaining these systems, you not only improve your productivity but also ensure tasks are completed more efficiently and effectively. As a result, you can stay focused on your goals, reduce stress, and enhance your overall performance in the workplace.

Develop Intentional Time to Grow

Growth in any area of expertise does not happen by chance—it requires a dedicated and intentional strategy. To truly enhance your performance, it is crucial to set aside time that is specifically focused on personal and professional development. This intentional time is a proactive investment in honing your skills, expanding your knowledge, and becoming more effective in your role.

Action Step: Start by identifying the areas where growth is most needed. This step takes some honest reflection and personal assessment. Consider feedback from peers or trusted advisors or consider new demands in your field that highlight where you can improve. Once you have identified those areas, develop a structured plan that includes setting clear goals, outlining the steps necessary to achieve them, and scheduling consistent time blocks dedicated to this growth.

Action Step: Use your intentional time wisely. Whether it's enrolling in relevant courses, attending workshops, seeking mentorship, or simply dedicating time for reading and research, make sure the activities you engage in are aligned with your growth objectives. Consistency is key—this cannot be a one-time effort but an ongoing commitment to self-improvement.

Equally important is reflecting on your progress regularly.

Action Step: Evaluate what's working and what needs adjustment to stay on track. Document your learnings and apply them in real-world scenarios to test and reinforce your development. Over time, this practice not only improves your performance in your current role but also prepares you for future opportunities and challenges.

Incorporating intentional time for growth into your routine ensures that you are not leaving your development to chance. It empowers you to take ownership of your professional journey, helping you become more skilled, knowledgeable, and ultimately, more successful in your field.

Use Feedback

Throughout my career, I used a tool for accepting and giving feedback called the BICA Feedback Model. BICA is a structured approach that focuses on specific BEHAVIORS, the IMPACT of those behaviors, any potential CONSEQUENCES if the behavior continues and provides suggestions or options for ALTERNATE BEHAVIORS.

- Behaviors: When giving feedback, it is important to focus on the behavior that occurred, observable actions. If feedback is delivered with assumptions, subjective judgements or perceptions, the receiver of the feedback is more likely to misunderstand the feedback or dispute the feedback. When the behavior is pointed out, the receiver will more than likely accept the feedback and be Willig to listen to the impact and next steps.

- Impact: Once the behaviors are identified, the next step is to describe the impact of those behaviors which helps the receiver understand that the feedback is real and has a negative impact.

- Consequences: If the behavior does not change, there could be consequences. It is important to redirect the behavior so that there is not a negative impact on the receiver or those around them.

- Alternate Behavior: It is important for the feedback giver to offer a suggestion or options for an alternate behavior that would be more effective in achieving the desired outcome. This provides a solution and empowers the person to take ownership and make positive changes.

Whether you are the feedback giver or the receiver, remember that FEEDBACK IS A GIFT and it must be given or received with the intent to make improvements and grow. Feedback should be delivered or received in a non-confrontational manner between people who have a trust relationship and share mutual respect. Feedback is a useful framework for leaders to foster open communication and continuous improvement.

Learn More About Top Performers

Top performers often develop strategies, routines and

approaches that lead to consistent success. Learning more about top performers can help you improve your performance. By studying high achievers, you can model their behaviors that led to that success.

- Mindset: High achievers and top performers typically have a growth mindset and a strong sense of purpose. They have well-defined goals and a strategy for how to achieve those goals. Understanding how to approach challenges, setbacks and even continuous learning can inspire you to adopt a similar mindset which can lead to enhanced personal and professional growth.

- Key Skills and Competencies: To be a high performer, you must master key skills and competencies. Examining the skill sets that top performers exhibit will allow you to target those areas for your own development. Obviously, the goal is not to mimic their behaviors but to enhance yours. You can identify any gaps that you may have in your own abilities and focus on closing those gaps.

- Work Ethic: It is critical to be reliable, dedicated, accountable, and have discipline and persistence to demonstrate a positive work ethic. A strong work ethic is one of the most important qualities for success, as it reflects an individual's commitment to their responsibilities and goals. Top performers must exhibit a positive work ethic since they must be reliable, consistently meeting deadlines and fulfilling promises. Reliability builds trust with colleagues and clients alike. Dedication plays a key role, as those who are fully invested in their tasks often go above and beyond, showing passion for their work and a willingness to put in extra effort when necessary. Accountability reflects ownership of your actions and outcomes – accepting responsibility for both successes and failures, learning from mistakes and striving for continuous improvement.

Demonstrating and modeling these qualities such as reliability, dedication, accountability, discipline, and persistence, embodies a positive work ethic that leads to personal and professional growth, while contributing to a collaborative and successful work environment.

Utilize Mentoring and Coaching

Mentoring is a powerful tool for personal and professional development, offering guidance, support, and inspiration for growth. The effectiveness of a mentor-mentee relationship lies in key principles that form the foundation of a successful partnership. Mentors serve as motivators, encouraging their mentees to pursue their passions and achieve their goals with dedication. They exemplify excellence, inspiring their mentees to strive for their best in all endeavors. Mentors also play a pivotal role in expanding the mentee's network, connecting them to valuable resources and opportunities. Investing time in building a strong, nurturing relationship ensures that mentees feel supported, while openness and trust create a safe environment for growth. Mutual respect, rooted in trust, solidifies the bond between mentor and mentee, ensuring a lasting and meaningful relationship. These principles help mentors guide their mentees toward success and fulfillment:

> M — Motivation: Mentors are motivators. They should be readily available and provide positive encouragement to help mentees pursue their passions and goals.
>
> E — Excellence: Mentors should exhibit excellence and should urge their mentees to do their absolute best in everything they do.
>
> N — Networking: Mentors should help mentees establish a strong network and, if possible, introduce them to influential people and to new networking opportunities.
>
> T — Time: Time together is important, and mentors should be willing to invest their time and establish a nurturing relationship. They should be willing to have regular meetings to establish a strong support system.
>
> O — Openness: Openness and trust between the mentor and mentee are critical, and if they are established early, the mentor/mentee relationship will thrive.
>
> R — Respect: Mutual respect ties into trust, and once a mentor relationship has been established, mutual respect will hold that relationship together.

Conclusion

Nurturing performance requires a multifaceted approach that combines organization, intentionality, feedback, learning from top performers, and mentoring **and** coaching. By staying organized, individuals can manage tasks efficiently and increase productivity. Intentional time set aside for personal growth and development fosters a clear strategy for continuous improvement. Effective feedback, such as the BICA model, helps refine behaviors and reinforce positive outcomes. Learning from top performers offers valuable insights into best practices and strategies that drive success. Finally, mentoring and coaching provide the motivation, support, and guidance needed to help individuals achieve excellence, develop strong networks, and maintain discipline in their professional journey. Together, these elements form a strong foundation for sustained personal and professional performance growth.

Denola M. Burton

PART 3: ACHIEVE

Denola M. Burton

CHAPTER 8: ACHIEVING PEAK PERFORMANCE IN LEADERSHIP

Leadership is not a destination but a journey of continuous evolution. To truly achieve peak performance as a leader, one must develop and nurture a mindset and behaviors that push boundaries, adapt to challenges and inspire growth. In this chapter, you will explore the essential components of achieving peak performance, starting with the mindset required to elevate your leadership abilities.

Growth Mindset vs. Fixed Mindset

At the core of leadership performance is the distinction between a growth mindset and a fixed mindset. A fixed mindset suggests that abilities and intelligence are static traits, whereas a growth mindset believes that skills and leadership capacities can always be improved through effort, learning, experiences and persistence.

Leaders with a growth mindset:

- Embrace challenges as opportunities for learning
- Persevere during setbacks, using them to fuel growth

- Value effort as the path to mastery

- Learn from criticism and feedback, constantly seeking improvement

- Find inspiration in the success of others, understanding that leadership is about elevating the collective

Conversely, leaders with a fixed mindset may avoid challenges, feel threatened by others' successes, or ignore our discount constructive feedback, which hinders their growth potential. Achieving peak leadership performance begins with embracing a growth mindset, ensuring that you never stop learning or striving for improvement.

Developing Core Leadership Competencies

Peak leadership performance requires the consistent honing of core competencies. These include strategic thinking, emotional intelligence, effective communication, adaptability, and decision-making skills. As a leader, mastering these competencies involves regular self-reflection, seeking mentorship, and participating in continuous education.

Key competencies to focus on include:

- Strategic Vision: Ability to set long-term goals and steer teams toward impactful outcomes.

- Emotional Intelligence: Understanding and managing

emotions—both yours and others—to build strong relationships.

- Communication: Clear, persuasive, and empathetic communication that inspires and aligns teams.

- Adaptability: Being flexible in the face of change and leading teams through uncertainty.

- Problem-Solving: Using critical thinking to navigate obstacles, make informed decisions, and implement solutions.

By continuously developing these core leadership traits, you will build the foundation for peak performance and positively influence those around you.

Health, Well-Being, and Sustainability

Peak leadership performance is not just about driving outcomes—it also involves maintaining balance in your physical, mental, and emotional health. Effective leaders prioritize self-care while performing at a high level. When you are mindful of your well-being, you are more resilient and better equipped to handle the pressures of leadership.

Strategies for sustaining well-being include:

- Mindfulness Practices: Incorporate meditation, journaling, or other mindfulness techniques to stay grounded and focused.

- Physical Health: Exercise regularly, eat a balanced

diet, and ensure proper rest to sustain your energy and focus. (Easier said than done, I get it!).

- Emotional Resilience: Practice emotional regulation, seek support when needed, and embrace vulnerability when faced with challenges.

Effective leaders must practice self-awareness to know when you need to recharge and ensure your approach to leadership is long-lasting rather than burning out from high stress.

Continuous Improvement

Leaders who achieve peak performance adopt the principles of continuous improvement. Just as top athletes never stop training, top leaders continually evaluate their performance, seek feedback, and look for ways to improve. Applying continuous improvement to your leadership requires both humility and ambition as well as a desire to improve the status quo combined with the ability to execute necessary changes.

Steps to incorporate continuous improvement:

- Solicit Feedback: Seek honest input from peers, mentors, and team members to understand your blind spots remembering that 'feedback is a gift'.

- Self-Reflection: Regularly assess your performance to identify strengths and areas for growth.

- Set Stretch Goals: Challenge yourself with goals that push you beyond your comfort zone.

- Celebrate Milestones: Recognize the small wins while keeping the bigger picture in focus.

By integrating continuous improvement into your leadership, you ensure that your growth journey never stalls.

Leadership Legacy and Impact

Peak performance isn't just about what you achieve in the moment; it's also about the legacy you leave behind. Leaders at the height of their abilities focus on the long-term impact they are creating, not just for themselves, but for the people and the organizations they serve. Building a leadership legacy means that the skills, values, and impact you've fostered will continue to benefit others long after you're gone.

Building a legacy involves:

- Mentoring and Developing Others: Empower others by sharing your knowledge, coaching, and giving back.

- Cultivating a Culture of Excellence: Foster an environment where continuous learning and high performance are valued.

- Long-Term Vision: Ensure that your leadership decisions consider future generations and leave a lasting positive impact.

- Purpose-Driven Leadership: Lead with values and a vision that transcends individual success, focusing on societal or organizational betterment.

Conclusion: Leadership as a Continuous Journey

Achieving peak performance in leadership is about constant growth, reflection, and adaptation. It requires commitment to your own development and a deep understanding of the evolving challenges and opportunities in leadership. By maintaining a growth mindset, continuously developing core competencies, prioritizing well-being, and striving for long-term impact, you will consistently elevate your leadership performance and inspire those you lead to achieve great things.

CHAPTER 9: ACHIEVING EXCELLENCE IN COMMUNICATION

Communication is more than just the words we speak or write, it's the key to building connections, trust, mutual respect and influence. Achieving excellence in communication requires a conscious effort to refine and evolve how we interact with others. It involves understanding that communication is a two-way effort where listening and responding appropriately are just as important as speaking clearly.

Growth Mindset vs. Fixed Mindset in Communication

When leaders have a growth mindset in communication, they see communication as a skill that can continuously improve. They seek feedback, learn from past interactions and embrace challenges in communication. This may include navigating through tough conversations or adapting to different audiences. A fixed mindset sees communication as an inherent skill, leading to missed opportunities for development. To achieve excellence, leaders must be open to learning and growing through every communication experience.

Health, Well-being and Sustainability in Communication

Peak performance in communication can only be achieved when leaders are mindful of their health and well-being. Communication fatigue is real, especially in high-stakes environments where constant interaction is required. Taking care of mental and emotional health helps leaders sustain the energy needed to communicate effectively. Building healthy boundaries, engaging in self-reflection, and prioritizing rest are all critical for maintaining excellence in communication over time.

Continuous Improvement

The most effective leaders leave behind a communication legacy—whether it's the culture of open communication they foster, the emotional intelligence they model, or the clarity they bring to complex discussions. Leaders striving for performance excellence should consider how their communication shapes their team, organization, and even their industry. They need to consider the lasting impact of their words and how can they continue to refine their message to align with their long-term vision.

Conclusion

By mastering these principles and embracing a mindset of continuous growth, leaders can achieve communication excellence, building stronger relationships, solving problems more effectively, and ultimately driving greater impact in their organizations and communities.

CHAPTER 10: ACHIEVING PERFORMANCE EXCELLENCE

We have covered many of the essential points related to achieving performance excellence. However, to ensure completeness, let's discuss a few corporate examples where the Enhanced DNA Framework fosters performance excellence.

Google: A Culture of Continuous Improvement

Google is an American multinational corporation and technology company focusing on online advertising, search engine technology, cloud computing, computer software, quantum computing, e-commerce, consumer electronics, and artificial intelligence. Google relies on "people analytics" to align personal performance with company goals. This focus on nurturing innovation and open communication has driven their consistent global success and has led to Google consistently being ranked high on *Fortune's* Best Companies to Work For list.

Google is renowned for its focus on innovation and high performance. Their culture promotes continuous learning and improvement, which drives their global success.

- **Develop**: Google emphasizes personal development, offering employees 20% of their time to work on passion projects that align with company goals. This encourages innovation and leadership.

- **Nurture**: The organization fosters open communication through initiatives like "TGIF," a company-wide Q&A where employees can ask leadership questions.

- **Achieve**: They track and celebrate high performance through clear goal-setting frameworks, such as **OKRs (Objectives and Key Results)**, to align personal performance with company objectives.

Google's focus on transparency, development opportunities, and clear goal alignment illustrates how a nurturing environment leads to performance excellence.

Southwest Airlines: Building Performance through Employee-Centric Leadership

Southwest Airlines, a major airline in the United States that operates on a low-cost carrier model, achieves operational excellence by prioritizing employee well-being. Through leadership that nurtures a family-like atmosphere and extensive professional development, Southwest empowers employees to deliver outstanding customer service, which translates into high performance and profitability. Southwest drives a positive employee culture in all aspects of their business, taking care of their people and their communities.

Southwest Airlines has long been praised for its customer service and strong operational performance, which can be traced back to its leadership philosophy that prioritizes employee well-being.

- **Develop**: Southwest invests heavily in training and professional development, ensuring employees have the tools they need to perform their roles at a high level.

- **Nurture**: The airline's leadership fosters a family-like atmosphere, emphasizing trust and empowerment, which enables staff to go above and beyond in customer service.

- **Achieve**: This people-first strategy directly translates to operational excellence, helping Southwest consistently outperform competitors in customer satisfaction and profitability.

Southwest Airlines showcases how nurturing employees and focusing on their development can result in excellent customer service and overall business success.

Toyota: Achieving Excellence through Kaizen (Continuous Improvement)

Toyota, one of the largest automotive companies in the world has a Kaizen philosophy of continuous improvement which is a hallmark of their success. By encouraging employees at all levels to focus on problem-solving and process optimization, Toyota has achieved superior quality control and production efficiency, solidifying its status as a global leader. In fact, the Toyota culture is described as "producing happiness for all" and focuses on 10 key values to make a positive impact for employees and those they serve.

Toyota's performance management model, **Kaizen**, is one of the most well-known examples of continuous improvement. It is a key driver of their success and ability to stay competitive in the automotive industry.

- **Develop**: Toyota encourages employees at all levels to continuously seek ways to improve processes, highlighting how developing problem-solving skills is essential for performance.

- **Nurture**: Their focus on teamwork and open communication between employees and managers creates a nurturing environment where every team member feels heard.

- **Achieve**: The Kaizen mindset leads to superior quality control, cost efficiency, and production speed, which have established Toyota as a global leader in performance excellence.

Toyota's structured approach to development and nurturing its workforce fosters continuous improvements that drive long-term performance excellence.

Conclusion

Each of these organizations demonstrates how developing

talent, nurturing relationships, and striving for excellence are essential to achieving high performance, making them powerful examples of the Enhanced DNA Framework in action.

Denola M. Burton

PART 4: PRACTICAL APPLICATION

Denola M. Burton

CHAPTER 11: TAKING ACTION

Throughout this book, we've explored how to develop, nurture, and ultimately achieve success in leadership, communication, and performance, both personally and professionally. This approach forms the core of the Enhanced DNA Framework. Now, let's dive into some practical applications that you can implement, organized under each key theme.

Developing Leadership Excellence

- **Self-Assessment Tools**: Utilize 360-degree feedback, leadership assessments (like DISC, StrengthsFinder), or personality tests (like MBTI) to identify leadership strengths and areas for growth.

- **Setting Leadership Goals**: Use the SMAART Goals Framework to set specific, measurable leadership development goals, ensuring alignment with both personal values and organizational objectives.

- **Mentorship Programs**: Engage in mentorship, either as a mentor or mentee, to learn leadership skills through real-life experiences. This facilitates learning from others' successes and failures.

- **Delegation Practice**: Start small by delegating tasks and responsibilities, then gradually increase the complexity of delegation to build trust and leadership acumen.

Nurturing Your Leadership Skills

- **Regular Reflection**: Set aside time weekly to reflect on leadership experiences, challenges, and accomplishments. Journaling can help track growth and identify patterns in decision-making.

- **Continuous Learning**: Engage in leadership seminars, conferences, or online courses to keep up with new leadership theories and trends. Books on transformational leadership or emotional intelligence can also be valuable.

- **Feedback Loops**: Establish a system for receiving ongoing feedback from team members, peers, and supervisors to adjust and nurture leadership skills.

- **Community Engagement**: Volunteering to lead initiatives outside the workplace fosters community leadership and develops the ability to lead diverse groups.

Achieving Leadership Excellence

- **Cross-Functional Projects**: Take on cross-functional or organization-wide projects to apply and test leadership skills in various environments, building a stronger leadership foundation.

- **Leadership Legacy Plan**: Create a long-term vision of how you want to be remembered as a leader. Focus on the impact you want to have on your team, organization, and community.

- **Succession Planning**: As a senior leader, mentor and develop your team's next generation of leaders to ensure leadership continuity.

Developing Your Communication Skills

- **Active Listening**: Engage in active listening exercises, focusing on paraphrasing, clarifying, and validating what others say. This skill can be honed in meetings or one-on-one conversations.

- **Effective Feedback**: Practice the BICA feedback model (Behavior, Impact, Consequence, Alternative) when giving feedback to others to ensure it is constructive and forward-focused.

- **Public Speaking Engagements**: Start with small-scale presentations to practice communicating ideas clearly and effectively. Gradually work up to more formal settings or larger audiences.

Nurturing Your Communication Skills

- **Relationship Building**: Spend time getting to know your team members or stakeholders on a personal level. This helps foster trust and mutual respect and makes communication more fluid and effective.

- **Cultural Competence**: Participate in cross-cultural communication training to learn how to effectively communicate with people from different backgrounds and cultures.

- **Non-Verbal Communication**: Improve body language awareness through mirror exercises or recording presentations to review gestures, posture, and facial expressions.

Achieving Communication Excellence

- **Coaching for Communication Skills**: Engage in professional coaching to focus on overcoming communication barriers or improving public speaking skills.

- **Negotiation Training**: Take part in workshops or role-playing scenarios that help refine persuasive communication, particularly in negotiation settings.

- **Storytelling for Leadership**: Develop the ability to communicate key messages through storytelling. This helps engage and inspire your audience while making communication memorable.

Developing Performance Excellence

- **Set Performance Goals**: Using the SMAART framework, set clear goals tied to organizational and personal benchmarks. Make sure to include milestones and metrics to measure progress.

- **Skill Gap Analysis**: Identify areas where skill development is needed and create a personal development plan (PDP) to address those gaps through targeted learning activities.

- **Time Management Techniques**: Use tools like time-blocking or the Pomodoro technique to structure your day and prioritize tasks more effectively.

Nurturing Your Performance

- **Focus on Well-Being**: Incorporate mindfulness, exercise, or mental health practices into your daily routine to ensure you're nurturing not only your performance but also your well-being.

- **Regular Performance Reviews**: Establish routine self-assessments or check-ins with a supervisor to assess performance against goals and adjust strategies as necessary.

- **Celebrate Small Wins**: Take time to acknowledge and celebrate minor achievements to maintain motivation and positive momentum.

Achieving Performance Excellence

- **Utilize Mentors or Coaches**: Work with a performance coach or mentor to help fine-tune performance strategies and address roadblocks.

- **Create Accountability Systems**: Partner with colleagues or mentors to create systems of accountability. This could involve regular progress updates or performance check-ins.

- **Benchmarking Success**: Compare your performance against industry or role-specific benchmarks to ensure you're reaching the highest standards in your field.

Conclusion

As you apply these strategies to enhance your leadership, communication, and performance expertise, remember that growth is a continuous process. Success doesn't happen overnight, but through consistent effort, self-reflection, and adaptation. The practical applications shared here are designed to serve as a roadmap to guide your journey. By integrating these principles into your daily routine, you will strengthen your DNA, enabling you to navigate challenges and seize opportunities with confidence, leading to sustained personal and professional achievement.

FINAL THOUGHTS

As we come to final thoughts, it is essential to reflect on the journey we have taken through the Enhanced DNA Framework. Much like our biological DNA shapes who we are physically, the Enhanced DNA Framework serves as a foundation for how we develop, nurture, and achieve success in leadership, communication, and performance.

We began by focusing on Developing - harnessing a growth mindset, embracing learning, and fostering core competencies that empower you to step into leadership. We then explored the importance of Nurturing - investing in self-care, continuous improvement, and building relationships that elevate your leadership capacity and communication. Finally, we delved into Achieving - where you apply all you've learned to reach peak performance, leaving a meaningful legacy through your impact and leadership.

Throughout this journey, the core principles of leadership, communication, and performance have been intertwined, creating a comprehensive roadmap for success. By intentionally developing these areas, nurturing them through reflection and growth, and striving to achieve your fullest potential, you not only enhance yourself but also inspire and elevate those around you.

The Enhanced DNA Framework is not a one-time solution; it is a process of ongoing refinement. As you continue your personal and professional journey, remember that true success comes from the continuous evolution of who you are and what you do. The tools, strategies, and insights shared in this book are here to guide you in becoming the best version of yourself, one that is adaptable, resilient, and empowered to make a lasting impact.

To your continued growth and success. May you always strive to enhance your DNA and live a life of purpose, achievement, and excellence.

ABOUT THE AUTHOR

Denola M. Burton is the Founder and CEO of *Enhanced DNA: Develop Nurture Achieve, LLC*. Denola holds the Bachelor and Master of Science degrees in Biology. After beginning her career as a scientist, she transitioned into Human Resources and maintains certifications as a Professional in Human Resources from both the *Society for Human Resource Management (SHRM-CP)*, and the *Human Resource Certification Institute (HRCI-PHR)*. She is a Certified DISC Behavioral Coach through *Innermetrix North America* and is a Certified Speaker, Trainer, Coach with the *John Maxwell Team*.

Through *Enhanced DNA: Develop Nurture Achieve*, Denola develops and nurtures individuals and organizations to enhance their Leadership, Communication and Performance "DNA." Denola is an author and a publisher and is a member of the Independent Book Publishers Association (IBPA). In 2019, Denola created Enhanced DNA Publishing and uses the Enhanced DNA Framework to develop and nurture authors so they can achieve their goals as a published author.

Denola retired in December 2017 from Eli Lilly and Company where her career spanned over 27 years. She has been married to her husband, Phillip, for over 31 years and they have two daughters, Danielle and Ciara.

Connect with Denola:

Email	info@EnhancedDNA1.com
Website	www.DevelopNurtureAchieve.com
	www.EnhancedDNAPublishing.com
LinkedIn	Denola Burton and Enhanced DNA Publishing
Facebook	Enhanced DNA: Develop Nurture Achieve, Enhanced DNA Publishing and Road to AUTHORity Page
Instagram	@Enhanced_DNA

Want to become a published author? Check out the award-winning book:

Enhancing Your Author DNA: Step-By-Step Publishing Guide
Denola M. Burton

Book Summary:

Enhancing Your Author DNA: Step-By-Step Publishing Guide

You wrote the book! Now what? How do you get it published? What are the steps that you need to take to have a professionally published product? Should you self-publish? Do you need a professional? Are you overwhelmed?

In Enhancing Your Author DNA: Step-by-Step Publishing Guide, Denola M. Burton, author, publisher and Founder/CEO of Enhanced DNA: Develop Nurture Achieve, LLC and Enhanced DNA Publishing, provides a step-by-step process for you to understand the publishing process so that you can publish the right way. By identifying your "Author DNA" you will be able to understand your goals and achieve them.

This publishing guide provides details that every author needs to know, whether they self-publish or turn their manuscript over to a publisher. You will learn the steps required to meet the publishing standards set by the Independent Book Publishers Association (IBPA). In addition, you will receive the tools to create a publishing and a marketing plan to ensure that you stay on track. Whether you do it yourself or hire a professional, it is important for you to understand the basics of the process. This publishing guide will prepare you to make the right decisions to move you from writer to author!

Enhancing Your Leadership, Communication and Performance DNA

Want to learn how to Self-Publish your book? Check out the Enhanced DNA Publishing Academy.

Want to learn how to Self-Publish your book? Check out the Enhanced DNA Publishing Academy.

Want to learn more about Denola Burton and how you can book her services?

Denola M. Burton

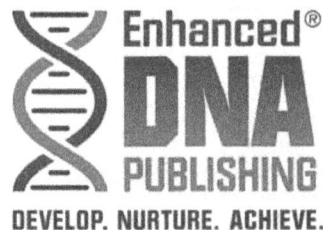

Enhanced DNA Publishing
DenolaBurton@EnhancedDNA1.com
317-537-1438

www.ingramcontent.com/pod-product-compliance
Lightning Source LLC
Chambersburg PA
CBHW050914160426
43194CB00011B/2409